Contents

Heat and Dust

Running in desert conditions is as tough as it gets. Yet athletes in the 'Marathon of the Sands' run 233 kilometres over six days across the Sahara. Loaded like packhorses, they carry everything they need in a rucksack weighing around 11 kilograms – and all in a 50ºC heat!

TO THE LIMIT

Extreme Sports

Jim Pipe

W

FRANKLIN WATTS
LONDON • SYDNEY

First published in 2014 by Franklin Watts

Copyright © Franklin Watts 2014

Franklin Watts
338 Euston Road
London NW1 3BH

Franklin Watts Australia
Level 17/207 Kent Street
Sydney, NSW 2000

Produced for Franklin Watts by White-Thomson Publishing Ltd

www.wtpub.co.uk
+44 (0) 843 208 7460

Edited and designed by Paul Manning

A CIP catalogue record for this book is available from the British Library.

Dewey no: 796'.046
Hardback ISBN: 978 1 4451 3426 0
Library eBook ISBN: 978 1 4451 3650 9

Printed in China

Franklin Watts is a division of Hachette Children's Books,
an Hachette UK company.
www.hachette.co.uk

Picture credits:
Front cover, Shutterstock/Atlaspix; 3,5, Corbis; 6, Corbis/Christophe Dupont Elise/Icon SMI;
7, courtesy Mauro Prosperi; 8, Corbis/Troy Wayrynen; 9, Andy Jones/Cycling Weekly;
10, Ullsteinbild/TopFoto; 12, Corbis/Arne Dedert; 13, courtesy Hamiltonpostcards.com;
14, Corbis/Elizabeth Kreutz; 15, Corbis/Karl-Josef Hildenbrand; 16, Corbis/Nic Bothma;
17, Photolibrary/Norbert Eisele-Hein; 18, courtesy Martin Strel; 19, Shutterstock/Peter
Jochems; 20, Photolibrary/Jochen Tack; 21, Shutterstock/Logan Carter; 22, Corbis/Franck
Seguin/Deadline Photo Press; 23, Getty images; 23, Corbis; 24, Willy Boykens,
Jumpforthecause.com; 25, Shutterstock/Drazen Vukelic; 26, Getty/Barcroft Media.

Every attempt has been made to clear copyright. Should there be any inadvertent
omission please apply to the publisher for rectification.

Hey there! Before reading this book, it's really important for you to know
that the extreme sports shown in it are meant for you to enjoy reading and
for no other purpose. The activities depicted are really dangerous; trying
to do them could hurt or even kill people. They should only be done by
professionals who have had a lot of training and, even then, they are still
really dangerous and can cause injury. So we don't encourage you to try
any of these activities. Just enjoy the read!

In 1994, Italian policeman Mauro Prosperi (right) entered the desert marathon known as 'the toughest foot race on Earth'. Though he was an experienced athlete, this was his first competition in the desert. By the third day, he was in seventh place and going well.

At the 32-kilometre mark, he reached the checkpoint where runners were given water, and set off again. Then the wind started to blow. For six hours, a fierce sandstorm swept across the desert. Soon Mauro was lost. He kept running, but further and further in the wrong direction.

Going bats

Mauro decided to wait for help. A helicopter buzzed over his head, but no one saw him. To stay alive, he rested in the shade of cliffs during the day. On cold nights, he buried his body in the sand. He drank his own urine and ate bats, snakes and lizards – raw!

◀ *In the gruelling third stage of the 2007 Marathon of the Sands, contestants face midday temperatures of up to 120°C. Roughly three-quarters of the distance is over rough, stony ground like this; the rest is over sand dunes.*

After nine days in the desert, Mauro was found by shepherds. The local police thought he was a spy and took him to the town of Algiers. He was 300 kilometres off-route, and had lost over 14 kilograms in weight. But he was still alive.

Hero's welcome

Mauro Prosperi became a hero back in Italy and was nicknamed the 'Robinson Crusoe of the Sahara'. Though it took him a year to recover, he was soon back for more. In his own words: 'It was a terrible experience and yet it was a great one. I love nature and I love the desert; I could not stay apart from it too long; that's why I'm back.'

'ULTRA MARATHONS'

Ultra marathons are races that are more than 50 kilometres long. In Antarctica, a 100-kilometre ultra marathon is held where temperatures drop to −20ºC. 'Adventure marathons' combine running with whitewater canoeing, mountain climbing, skiing and even caving.

Wheels on Fire

To perform incredible stunts like somersaulting through the air or spinning a bike through 720°, BMX athletes need the powerful legs of a racer, the balance of an acrobat and the nerves of a daredevil. Shanaze Reade showed she had all three when the rough and tumble of BMX came to the Olympic Games in Beijing in 2008.

▶ Elite BMX rider Shanaze Reade of Great Britain leads the field in a qualifying round of the 2007 UCI BMX World Championships in Canada.

Twenty-two year-old British cyclist Shanaze Reade was hot favourite to win in the 2008 Olympic BMX women's event. She started riding when she was ten, taking her bike out on to the streets and often beating the boys in races. By 2007, Shanaze had won the senior women's world championship – and in 2008 she won it again.

Why did you choose BMX?

'It chose me! My uncle took me to a local BMX track and it has been a rollercoaster from then on. When I was 11, I won the first European championships I entered.'

Why do you compete in track cycling?

'I did track cycling to prove that BMX cyclists weren't just people on kids' bikes and to show that we are athletes.'

What's it like to beat the boys?

'It's competition. I suppose they hate it, but I think they keep it quiet so that it doesn't create a show.'

Do you get injured much?

'I've broken my foot twice, broken my wrist, dislocated both shoulders, broken my knee... That's nothing, really. When I broke my foot, I jumped back up and tried to finish the race'.

What's your goal?

'I want to get the best out of myself and I won't stop going until I achieve everything I can in the sport'.

BEIJING OR BUST

At the Beijing Olympics in 2008 Shanaze made it into the final, but her gamble to win a gold ended in blood and bruises – she crashed into the back wheel of another competitor while trying to pass her on the final bend. The result of all her efforts was a badly sprained wrist and a damaged shoulder to add to the injuries from earlier crashes.

Urban Tumble

▶ In Parkour, speed and agility are everything. It's down the fire escape, over the nearest wall and off to the next obstacle… fast!

Technically, Parkour is the art of getting from one place to another in a straight line – whatever obstacle gets in your way. Skilled exponents turn the city streets into a crazy playground, leaping walls, balancing cat-like on ledges and performing death-

The man who dreamed up the spectacular sport of Parkour was Frenchman David Belle. David's father Raymond served in the fire service in Paris, France. A born athlete, Raymond was an expert rope-climber and joined an elite team of fire-fighters who were always selected for the toughest missions.

Inspired by his father's heroic rescues, David always loved athletics, gymnastics and martial arts. Later, he joined the army and, like his father, became a champion rope-climber. But the strict army life was not for David.

The Yamakasi

In 1997, David formed a group called Yamakasi with a group of old friends dedicated to Parkour. The area of Paris they lived in, Lisses, was a perfect playground to learn moves and try out jumps. They also adapted rolls from martial arts that helped them land safely.

Martial art

Parkour can be spectacular. But it isn't about showing off. Like David, you need the balance and strength of a gymnast, the agility of a cat and the self-control of a martial arts expert. You imagine someone is chasing you, then you move in a way that gets you at top speed from A to B. Easy to understand – harder to perform!

FIGHTING FIT

Parkour became famous after a member of the original Yamakasi group, Sébastien Foucan, performed a series of amazing stunts in the opening scene of the James Bond movie Casino Royale. After hearing about it, military units such as the British Royal Marines were soon clamouring to use Parkour in their training.

Fly on the Wall

Scaling a tall building with ropes and climbing gear is crazy enough, but urban climbers set out with little more than a trusty pair of shoes and some chalk to help them grip the surface of a wall. Climbing alone and without ropes means they are either very good – or very dead!

⬤ Using only the most basic harness, world-famous French freeclimber Alain 'Spiderman' Robert scales the 166 metre-high Dresdner Bank tower in Frankfurt, Germany. Robert has so far climbed more than 70 skyscrapers and other international landmarks, including the Eiffel Tower in Paris and the Petronas Twin Towers in Kuala Lumpur, Malaysia.

Many urban climbers spend years developing their skills. For some, however, climbing a tall building is a sudden mad rush of blood to the head.

Shanghai Tower

On 18 February 2001, Han Qizhi was walking past the 88-storey Jin Mao Tower in Shanghai with a friend, when he felt a sudden overwhelming urge to climb it.

Han waited until the security guards were looking the other way, then dropped his jacket and began to clamber up the side of the building in his ordinary office clothes. Gripping the steel grid that encases the building, Han safely made it to the top despite the high winds, freezing temperatures and swirling fog.

Publicity stunt

Amazingly, although Han was in good shape, he had never climbed before. Why did he do it? A shoe salesman from the Chinese city of Hefei, he hoped his stunt would create some free publicity for his business.

Not everyone was impressed. Alain Robert, the French 'Spiderman' famous for clambering up the Eiffel Tower, had wanted to scale the tower first. 'My six-year-old son could climb that,' he sniffed, 'And I could do it with one arm!'

THE HUMAN FLY

The first famous urban climber was Harry H. Gardiner, known as the 'Human Fly'. He climbed over 700 buildings in Europe and North America in the early 20th century, usually wearing just his everyday clothes, tennis shoes and his spectacles.

▶ *This postcard shows Harry H. Gardiner climbing the Bank of Hamilton building in Washington DC, USA, on 11 November 1918, to celebrate the end of the First World War.*

Extreme Snurfing

Snowboarding and extreme stunts go hand in hand, from US pioneer Mike Basich's astonishing snowboard jump out of a helicopter 35 metres above the ground, to Frenchman Marco Siffredi's 5,300-metre ride down the North Face of Mount Everest in 2001. But how did it all start?

Canadian snowboarder Vallée Dominique catches some air during the 2006 Winter Olympics women's snowboard competition in Bardonecchia, Italy.

It was Christmas Day, 1965. Michigan engineer Sherman Poppen was watching his daughter standing up on her sled while sliding down a hill, when suddenly he had a brainwave. Sherman grabbed a pair of cheap skis and fixed them together – and the snowboard was born!

Sherman's wife came up with a name – 'Snurfer' – by combining the words 'snow' and 'surf'. The board looked like a lot of fun and snurfing was an instant hit. Sherman remembers young neighbours pestering him, 'Make me one, make me one!'

Freeriders

Sherman never imagined how popular his invention would become. Though snowboarding didn't really take off until the late 1980s, it's now the most popular winter sport in the world. Freeriders use the whole mountain, riding in deep powder snow, while freestylers copy skateboarding and surfing tricks.

Today extreme sports stars compete in 'big air' contests on specially built jumps. There are also 'extreme' riding contests down incredibly steep hills. Sherman doesn't snurf himself. But he still gets a kick out of passing a group of excited snowboarders.

SPEED SKIING

The fastest snowboarders can scream down a mountain at 200 kph. But speed skiers are even faster, reaching speeds of 240 kph. That's about as fast as you can go without an engine!

▶ Finnish skier Tanja Poutiainen speeds down the slope during the women's giant slalom at the Ski World Cup in Soelden. Austria

Wipeout!

For a novice, riding a surfboard can feel a bit like trying to stand up on a galloping horse. But extreme surfers can perform spectacular moves riding on waves that are taller than a four-storey building!

▼ A surfer rides a giant wave at Dungeons offshore reef near Cape Town, South Africa, 17 May 2009.

Surfing big waves is getting more and more popular. But monster waves are full of danger, as Australian surfer Kerby Brown found out in November 2008. Deep-sea fishermen had told Kerby and his friends about some amazing waves they had seen at a secret location off the south-west coast of Australia. The surfers decided to ride out to the spot on their jet skis.

'We sat and waited for a long time,' said Kerby. Then, about an hour before sunset, Kerby spotted his chance and went for it. Soon he was hurtling along on the largest wave he had ever seen. 'It was not like any other wave I've ridden. It was a dark, evil wave – the hardest wave I've ever had to surf. '

Dumped by a wave

Suddenly, the wave crashed down on Kerby, smashing him against a rocky shelf just below the surface. After flipping and doing a few somersaults, Kerby found himself being pushed deep underwater. 'I couldn't see the surface, I was so deep down.'

By the time he reached the surface, Kerby's lungs were fit to burst. Luckily, his brother was nearby and dragged him up onto his jet ski. Kerby was lucky to paddle away with just a few torn shoulder muscles.

KITESURFING

Wind power can be used to pull a kitesurfer through the water at incredible speed – up to 93 kph. The wing-like sails also allow kitesurfers to make spectacular jumps known as 'big steps'.

▶ Most kitesurfing takes place along ocean shores, usually off beaches, but kitesurfers also use large lakes and inlets and even rivers.

Big River Man

More than 800 people have swum the English Channel, but few swimmers can match the remarkable achievements of 'Big River Man' Martin Strel. In April 2007, the 53-year-old from Slovenia swam 5,268 kilometres down the Amazon River in just 66 days!

▼ *Swimming the Amazon River is like running a marathon every day for two months – with the added attraction of insects, piranha fish and crocodiles. It took Martin more than a year and a half to train for the swim – and seven months to recover. His motto is 'swimming for peace, friendship and clean waters'.*

MARTIN STREL, RECORD-BREAKER

1997 First to swim Africa to Europe, covering 78 kilometres in less than 30 hours.

2000 Swam the Danube, covering 3,004 kilometres in 58 days.

2002 Swam the Mississippi River, USA, a distance of 3,797 kilometres, in 68 days.

2004 Broke his own long-distance record, swimming 4,003 kilometres down the Yangtze River, China, in 51 days.

Martin Strel taught himself to swim when he was six and became a professional marathon swimmer in 1978. He has made record-breaking swims along some of the world's most famous rivers, but swimming the Amazon River was his biggest challenge ever.

How do you prepare for a swim?

'I train two times a day for three to five hours. During the swim itself, I eat lots of soup and pasta and drink at least 10 litres of fluid a day.'

Why was the Amazon so difficult?

'The water is muddy and you can't see anything.'

Bugs and scorpions

Setting off from jungle deep in Peru, Martin swam across Brazil to Bélem on the Atlantic coast. He wore a pillowcase mask to shield his face from the fierce sun and a wetsuit to protect him from animal bites.

He needed it. Spiders and scorpions dropped on to him from overhanging trees. Larvae burrowed under his skin. Wasp stings made his head buzz, and birds flew down to peck his face.

Sharks and piranhas

Martin swam the final 10 kilometres to Bélem in the dark. Despite the risk that lights on the safety boat would attract sharks, he made it safely to dry land.

How did you stay alive?

'On the boat alongside me I had two armed guards in case pirates attacked. They had buckets of flesh and blood ready to throw in the water to distract the piranhas. I knew I had to swim 12 hours a day and cover 80 kilometres. So I would talk to myself. I had to be stronger than the Amazon.'

▼ *Deadly flesh-eating piranha fish were just one of the hazards Martin faced during his epic swim down the Amazon River.*

Thrills and Spills

Just 15 centimetres of fast-flowing water can knock you off your feet, so imagine the power of a raging river, or 'white water'. Yet despite the danger, every year people risk life and limb to experience the thrill of shooting the rapids in a raft or canoe.

▼ Whitewater rafting calls for lightning reactions – especially when avoiding hazards like fallen trees or submerged boulders.

Lars Holbek was one of the most famous canoeists in the world. He first paddled at 16, canoeing down swollen creeks on his high school lunch break. On his first trip, Lars wore no lifejacket, no helmet, and no paddling jacket. But an early brush with danger taught him to respect the power of fast-flowing water.

Whitewater skills

One weekend, Lars headed off to test his whitewater skills in the wilderness of Idaho, a favourite spot for rafters and canoeists. Unpacking his canoe, Lars headed down the Golden Canyon in the Clearwater River. Swept downstream by the waters, he plunged straight into a huge 'hole' of swirling water.

Sucked underwater

Lars quickly wriggled free of his canoe and tried swimming downstream. But again and again he was sucked back into the hole. He knew he had to try something else or he was in real trouble. So he swam directly into the hole. He bounced along the bottom of the river, then slowly rose to the surface and made it to the shore.

It was a lucky escape. Later, he discovered his fibreglass boat mangled in the rocks downstream.

WATERFALL PLUNGE

Some canoeists go out of their way to find danger. In April 2009, Tyler Bradt paddled his kayak over the thundering 57 metre-high Palouse Falls in Washington State, USA. His kayak plunged 6 metres down in the pool at the bottom. Though he was underwater for about seven seconds, Tyler surfaced with little more than a sprained wrist.

57 metres

▶ The dramatic Palouse Falls in south-east Washington State, USA.

In at The Deep End

Many people have experienced the thrill of diving down below the waves, but very few have reached depths of 120 metres or more – without oxygen!

▶ In competitive freediving, the aim is to reach the greatest possible depth, time or distance, without the use of breathing equipment. It can be very risky. In deep water there's a huge pressure on your lungs and a very real danger of losing consciousness on the way up.

'Monofin' helps propel the diver through the water.

Undulating movement known as the 'dolphin kick' starts in the shoulders and ripples down the body.

Swimmer extends arms forward, clasping hands together and locking the head between the biceps.

In 2003, Tanya Streeter, the champion British free-diver (right), took a deep breath and plunged 121 metres into the deep, using only a giant monofin flipper. Three minutes 38 seconds later, she burst back onto the surface.

On the seabed, the water is dark and very lonely. It's a scary place. Tanya explained how important it is to stay calm and alert: 'I know that I have to touch down and head back up again immediately.'

Though Tanya had enjoyed snorkelling since she was young, she only began freediving six years before. For a record attempt, she trains for three months. She does weights while holding her breath, and swims underwater laps in a pool.

Tanya was very aware of the risks of diving so deep. A few months before, her arch-rival Audrey Mestre died while trying to set a new record. When Tanya broke the world record, there were 14 safety divers close by, Tanya explained: 'I'm a chicken and I simply wouldn't do it if I thought it was dangerous.'

▼ *Freediver Jaques Mayol (1927–2001) was the first to descend to 100 metres and was the holder of many other world freediving records.*

THE HUMAN DOLPHIN

Frenchman Jacques Mayol (right) was one of the great pioneers of freediving. While working in an aquarium in Florida in 1955, he met a female dolphin called 'Clown'. Imitating Clown, Mayol learned how to hold his breath and slow his heartbeat, just like a dolphin or seal.

The Sky's the Limit

Leaping out of a plane and hurtling towards the ground at 190 kph is the ultimate adrenaline rush. These days most skydiving is fairly safe. But it gets a lot more extreme when you're doing it with hundreds of other people at the same time!

Basic skydiving skills can be taught in a day. You jump out of the plane, pull the ripcord to open your 'chute, and gravity does the rest. But getting 440 skydivers to link up in the air as they plummet towards the ground is something else.

Mass skydive

It's February 2006. The World Team have gathered in Thailand to beat the record for the world's largest mass skydive. These are not just young thrill-seekers – the oldest jumper is 65. Many of them have jumped several thousand times. They'll need all their experience today.

◀ In the skies above California, USA, 81 female skydivers link up to set a new world record for the largest all-female skydiving formation.

Flying high

Five planes take to the sky in a 'V' formation, climbing high above the clouds. This gives around 100 seconds for everyone to link up. The skydivers leave the plane at a speed of 350 kph. The sudden blast of cold, clean air helps them to keep their wits about them. A mid-air bump with another skydiver could jolt an arm bone out of its socket.

It takes a week of practice to get everything right. Slowly, the number of jumpers linking up grows, from 100 to 200 to 300. Then, on jump number nine, everything comes together. Four hundred and forty skydivers link arms to form a giant frisbee shape. They hold on for 4.3 seconds – a new world record!

▶ The latest hang-gliders are able to glide for hundreds of kilometres in a single flight.

HANG-GLIDING RECORD

Hang-gliding is about as close as you can get to flying like a bird. Hang-gliders have travelled over 480 kilometres in one flight, and in 1985, US flyer Larry Tudor reached a height of 4,343 metres. Expert flyers can do all sorts of stunts from barrel rolls to flying upside down.

Free Fall

Most extreme sports are risky. Some are so dangerous, they're against the law. BASE jumping is top of the list. This mad sport is all about leaping off high buildings and rocks. Then it's a race to open your parachute before you hit the ground.

Wearing specially adapted bodywear called wingsuits, husband and wife BASE jumpers Heather Swan and Glenn Singleman launch themselves from the summit of Mt Brento in northern Italy.

At 47, Heather Swan is no ordinary Australian mother. A world record-holding BASE jumper, she's also the other half of the only husband-and-wife BASE jumping team on the planet!

Upside down

Heather's world was turned upside down in 1998 when she married adventure-loving Glenn Singleman, 51. Glenn lived a double life, working as a hospital doctor during the week and throwing himself into extreme sports in his spare time.

At first, Heather stayed at home with the children and bit her nails while Glen went skydiving over the Australian outback. Then she decided it was time to join him.

Before long, Heather was completely hooked on her new life as a daredevil. Six years after her first skydive, she began BASE jumping.

World record

In 2006, the couple set a new world record for the highest-ever BASE jump, leaping off the 4,566 metre-high peak of Mt Meru in Tanzania in specially designed wingsuits.

Now the couple are planning to become a daredevil family. Heather and Glen's four children are all expecting to make their first skydive when they reach their 14th birthday!

CONQUERING FEAR

'It took me a long time to conquer my natural fear of throwing myself off mountains, but somehow BASE jumping seemed more real and more dangerous than a skydive. Plus you've the added danger of plummeting next to a jagged cliff face.'

Heather Swan

How Extreme Are You?

Could you snowboard down Everest, scale the Eiffel Tower or leap off a tall building? Try this easy-to-answer quiz.

1 You're hiking with friends when you come face to face with a giant wall of rock. Would you:

   a Shout 'Last one to the top is an idiot,' fling off your backpack and start scrambling up the cliff.

   b Put on your climbing gear – helmet, harness and ropes. After taking a good look at the rock face, rope yourself to a friend and start climbing slowly but steadily.

   c Look for an easier route. The lovely view from the top can wait for another day.

2 What's your idea of fun? Is it:

   a Diving off a waterfall.

   b Diving off a high board into a swimming pool.

   c Diving into bed.

3 You're paddling a canoe down a river when you see foaming white water up ahead. Would you:

   a Scream 'Yeee-hah!' and paddle as fast as you can downstream.

   b Paddle to the side of the river and check there isn't a waterfall ahead. Work out a good route through the rocks, and put on your helmet before giving it a go.

   c Regret not going for the 'lilo on the swimming pool' option that morning.

4 What's the furthest you'd run?

   a 500 kilometres across a scorching desert.

   b A marathon (that's around 42 kilometres).

   c Down to the local newsagent.

5 You've been snowboarding for a couple of hours and you feel like trying something different. Would you:

   a Set off an avalanche just to see if you can outrun it.

   b Head for the snowboard park to try out some new jumps and tricks.

   c Glide down to the nearest café for a cup of steaming hot chocolate.

CHECK YOUR SCORE

Mostly a's You're a born daredevil – but you may not survive very long!

Mostly b's Extreme sports may be for you – you enjoy the danger but you don't believe in taking unnecessary risks.

Mostly c's Probably best to stick to sports that aren't too extreme. Table tennis and snooker are fairly safe options.

Glossary

adrenaline chemical our bodies produce when we are excited or fearful

agility ability to move quickly and easily

barrel roll rotating movement performed by a plane or glider

BASE jumping BASE stands for four types of fixed objects you can jump from: building, antenna, span and Earth (cliff)

biceps large muscles in the upper arm

caving sport of exploring caves or potholes

creek a narrow, sheltered stretch of water

elite a select group of people

exponent person who can perform a special skill

freeclimbing sport of climbing rocks using only your hands, feet or other parts of the body

freediving swimming as deep as possible without using breathing gear

gallop the fastest pace a horse can go

hang-gliding sport in which a pilot steers a light, unpowered craft that glides on air currents

inlet a short stretch of water branching off a lake, sea or river

jet ski jet-propelled craft which skims across the water

kayak lightweight canoe with a watertight cover

kitesurfing sport of skimming the water while being pulled along by a kite

larva the stage before a creature such as a caterpillar metamorphoses

obstacle object that gets in the way of something or somebody

packhorse a horse used to carry heavy loads

paragliding sport in which a person is lifted into the air beneath a parachute

Parkour sport of moving fast over fixed obstacles using only hands and feet

piranha flesh-eating fish found in South America

rucksack a bag with two straps which you carry on your back

scorpion member of the spider family with a poisonous sting in the tail

slalom a ski race down a winding course marked out by poles

undulating moving with a wave-like motion

white water fast-flowing stretch of water in a river

wipeout a fall from a surfboard

Websites

www.bmx.transworld.net/
The latest news, articles, pictures and videos can all be found on this BMX website.

www.alainrobert.com
Website dedicated to French urban climber Alain Robert, *aka* Spiderman.

www.snowboarding.transworld.net
Great snowboarding site, with pictures, video clips and information.

Note to parents and teachers

Every effort has been made by the Publishers to ensure that the web sites in this book are suitable for children, that they are of the highest educational value, and that they contain no inappropriate or offensive material. However, because of the nature of the Internet, it is impossible to guarantee that the contents of these sites will not be altered. We strongly advise that Internet access is supervised by a responsible adult.

Index